# NBA's TOP 10
# GAMES

BY MATT TUSTISON

NBA's
TOP 10

SportsZone

An Imprint of Abdo Publishing
abdopublishing.com

10 9 8 7 6 5 4 3 2 1

**abdopublishing.com**

Published by Abdo Publishing, a division of ABDO, PO Box 398166, Minneapolis, Minnesota 55439. Copyright © 2019 by Abdo Consulting Group, Inc. International copyrights reserved in all countries. No part of this book may be reproduced in any form without written permission from the publisher. SportsZone™ is a trademark and logo of Abdo Publishing.

Printed in the United States of America, North Mankato, Minnesota
022018
092018

Cover Photo: Marcio Jose Sanchez/AP Images
Interior Photos: Kevin Terrell/AP Images, 4–5; Harold P. Matosian/AP Images, 6–7; Manny Millan/Sports Illustrated/Getty Images, 9, 15; Lynne Sladky/AP Images, 10, 11; Bettmann/Getty Images, 12–13, 20; Eric Risberg/AP Images, 16; Marcio Jose Sanchez/AP Images, 17; AP Images, 18, 21; Paul Vathis/AP Images, 19; Jeff Haynes/AFP/Getty Images, 23; Dick Raphael/Sports Illustrated/Getty Images, 24, 24–25, 26–27

Editor: Patrick Donnelly
Series Designer: Craig Hinton

**Library of Congress Control Number: 2017962575**

**Publisher's Cataloging-in-Publication Data**

Names: Tustison, Matt, author.
Title: NBA's top 10 games / by Matt Tustison.
Other titles: NBA's top ten games
Description: Minneapolis, Minnesota : Abdo Publishing, 2019. | Series: NBA's top 10 | Includes online resources and index.
Identifiers: ISBN 9781532114519 (lib.bdg.) | ISBN 9781532154348 (ebook)
Subjects: LCSH: Sports tournaments--Juvenile literature. | Basketball--Records--United States--Juvenile literature. | Basketball--History--Juvenile literature. | National Basketball Association--Juvenile literature.
Classification: DDC 796.323--dc23

# TABLE OF
# **CONTENTS**

# INTRODUCTION

The National Basketball Association (NBA) began play in 1946. Originally called the Basketball Association of America (BAA), the league adopted its new name when it merged with the rival National Basketball League (NBL) in 1949.

Its teams have played thousands of games. Each year the playoffs provide tense, exciting matchups. Countless games have come down to the final seconds.

So what makes a game one of the top 10 of all time? The greatest games usually have something big on the line. They often feature legendary players, remarkable plays, or thrilling finishes.

Some games even have a long-lasting impact on the sport. Read on to learn more about the best games in NBA history.

# 10

Elgin Baylor (22) blocks the reverse layup attempt by Boston's Bailey Howell in Game 7 of the 1969 NBA Finals. →

# CELTICS CAP A DYNASTY

When the 1968–69 regular season ended, the Boston Celtics' dynasty appeared to be over, too. The Celtics had won 10 of the previous 12 NBA championships. But they entered the 1969 playoffs as the fourth seed in the East after finishing the regular season 48–34.

Legendary center Bill Russell was the Celtics' player-coach. He turned 34 that season. Star guard Sam Jones was 35 years old. The team had gotten older, but it still played strong defense and was unselfish. As a result, Boston upset the Philadelphia 76ers and the New York Knicks in the playoffs.

Now the Celtics were back in the NBA Finals against their longtime rivals, the Los Angeles Lakers. The Celtics had beaten the Lakers in the Finals six times during their amazing run, including in 1968. But the Lakers had added star center Wilt Chamberlain to a roster that already featured Hall of Famers Jerry West and Elgin Baylor. They were expected to finally end Boston's reign.

The series went to a winner-take-all Game 7 in Los Angeles. Boston took a 17-point lead in the fourth quarter, but the Lakers rallied. The Celtics led 103–102 with less than two minutes

remaining when the ball was knocked toward Boston forward Don Nelson. His jumper from near the foul line just beat the shot clock. The ball kicked high off the back rim and dropped straight into the basket.

The Celtics held on for a 108–106 win and another title. West scored 42 points in a triple-double performance but was again denied an NBA title. A few months later, Russell retired as player. He won a remarkable 11 NBA championships in his 13 seasons, including one last unlikely run to the mountaintop in 1969.

# 09

Magic Johnson, *far right*, releases his game-winning baby hook over Robert Parish (00) and Kevin McHale in Game 4 of the 1987 NBA Finals.

# BABY SKYHOOK

Game 4 of the 1987 NBA Finals was a key point in the history of the great Lakers-Celtics rivalry. Entering that year's Finals, each team had won three titles in the 1980s. The winner of the 1987 Finals would get a leg up in being able to call itself the NBA's team of the decade.

The Lakers took a 2–1 series lead. In Game 4, the Celtics raced to a 16-point lead in the second half. But Los Angeles rallied to cut the deficit to one point at a loud Boston Garden.

Then it was time for some Magic. Lakers star Earvin "Magic" Johnson was one of the best passers in NBA history. But at 6 feet 9 inches tall, he also could take the ball inside and beat the best big men in the game.

With seven seconds left, Johnson dribbled inside the lane. Boston's 6-foot-10 forward Kevin McHale and 7-foot center Robert Parish were waiting for him. Johnson pulled up just inside the free-throw line and lofted a one-handed shot over his head. His "baby" skyhook floated just beyond the defenders' reach and swished in. Los Angeles grabbed a 107–106 lead on the shot that Johnson had learned from legendary center Kareem Abdul-Jabbar, his 40-year-old teammate.

The Celtics had one last chance. Star forward Larry Bird launched a long shot that came up short. The Lakers went on to beat the Celtics in six games.

# TEAMS OF THE '80s

Los Angeles and Boston met in the NBA Finals three times in the 1980s. The Lakers won twice, including the last series in 1987. The Johnson-led Lakers finished the decade with five titles, while Bird and the Celtics won three. The other champs in the 1980s were the Philadelphia 76ers (1983) and the Detroit Pistons (1989).

# 08

## HEAT REFUSE TO LOSE

LeBron James and the Miami Heat's bid to defend their NBA title in the 2013 Finals appeared to be doomed. The Heat trailed San Antonio by 10 points entering the fourth quarter of Game 6 in Miami. James had made just 3 of 12 shots from the field. A loss would give Tim Duncan and the Spurs a fifth crown in their fifth try in the Finals.

Miami rallied, but the Spurs' Manu Ginobili hit a free throw to make it 94–89 with only 28 seconds remaining. Heat players noticed that NBA officials had brought out yellow tape to block off the court for a postgame San Antonio trophy presentation.

**Tim Duncan and the Spurs had Dwyane Wade, *right*, and the Heat on the ropes in Game 6.**

Ray Allen (34) shoots a 3-pointer over San Antonio's Tony Parker. The shot tied Game 6 with 5.2 seconds remaining.

Not so fast. James hit a three-pointer with 20 seconds left to cut the deficit to two. San Antonio's Kawhi Leonard made one of two free-throw tries to put the Spurs back up by three points with 19 seconds left.

That gave Miami one last chance to tie it. James misfired on a long three-point try. But teammate Chris Bosh grabbed the rebound and passed the ball to Ray Allen. The 37-year-old sharpshooter backed up beyond the three-point line in the corner. He released a shot that swished through the hoop. The game was tied with 5.2 seconds left.

When the Spurs' Tony Parker missed a shot at the buzzer, it was on to overtime. James's short jumper with 1:43 left put the Heat ahead for good. Miami pulled out a hard-fought 103–100 victory.

James played the entire second half and overtime. At game's end, he had 32 points, 11 assists, and 10 rebounds. More importantly, the Heat went on to win Game 7 for their second consecutive title.

# 07

John Havlicek makes a
play against the 76ers
earlier in the 1965
Eastern Division finals.

→

# HAVLICEK MAKES HISTORY

**B**oston radio announcer Johnny Most was at the microphone when the Celtics played the Philadelphia 76ers in the 1965 Eastern Division finals. The sound clip of his raspy voice describing the closing seconds of Game 7 became an instant classic.

Most's call came at the end of a game between the six-time defending NBA champion Celtics and the Philadelphia 76ers. The Celtics' title run was in jeopardy of ending. Boston's lead had shrunk to 110–109. The 76ers had the ball with five seconds left. Sixers guard Hal Greer prepared to inbound the ball under his own basket. Greer sent a pass to forward Chet Walker, but Boston forward John Havlicek lunged into the passing lane.

"Havlicek steals it! Over to Sam Jones!" Most shouted. "Havlicek stole the ball! It's all over! Johnny Havlicek stole the ball!"

Havlicek had tipped the inbounds pass away from Walker and toward Jones. Jones then dribbled out the clock as Boston fans ran onto the court. The Celtics had advanced to the NBA Finals. They went on to beat the Los Angeles Lakers in five games for their seventh title in a row.

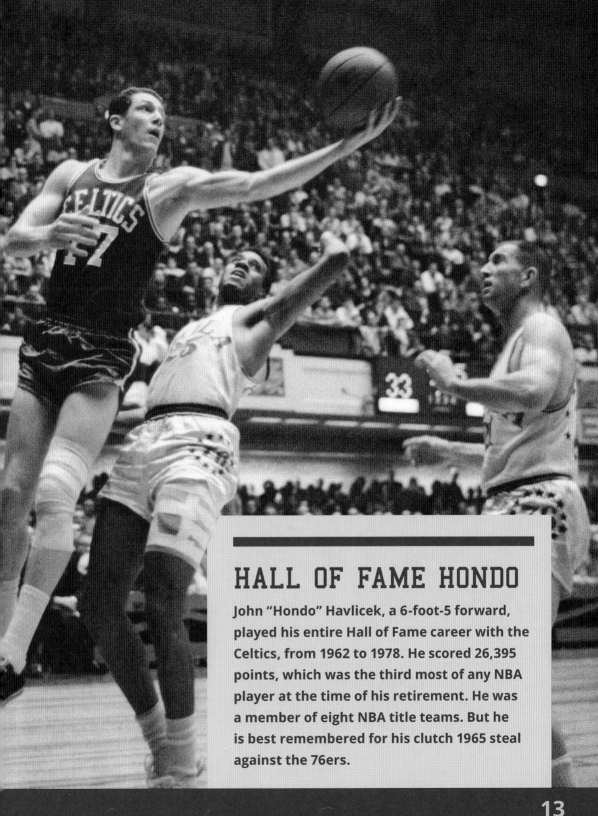

# HALL OF FAME HONDO

John "Hondo" Havlicek, a 6-foot-5 forward, played his entire Hall of Fame career with the Celtics, from 1962 to 1978. He scored 26,395 points, which was the third most of any NBA player at the time of his retirement. He was a member of eight NBA title teams. But he is best remembered for his clutch 1965 steal against the 76ers.

# 06

# MAGIC FROM A ROOKIE

**E**arvin "Magic" Johnson lived up to his nickname in his rookie season with the Los Angeles Lakers. At no point was this more evident than in the deciding game of the 1980 NBA Finals against the Philadelphia 76ers.

NBA Most Valuable Player (MVP) Kareem Abdul-Jabbar suffered a sprained ankle in Los Angeles's Game 5 victory. The Lakers headed back to Philadelphia with a 3–2 series lead but without their star center.

Upon boarding the plane to Philadelphia, Johnson took Abdul-Jabbar's usual seat in the first row. He winked at coach Paul Westhead and announced to his Lakers teammates, "Never fear, E. J. is here!"

Johnson was a remarkable player in that he was 6 feet 9 inches tall but played point guard. In Game 6, however, the Lakers needed Johnson in the middle to replace Abdul-Jabbar. The rookie filled in for the MVP admirably. Johnson finished with 42 points, 15 rebounds, and seven assists. Veteran forward Jamaal Wilkes added 37 points as the Lakers surprised the 76ers and star forward Julius "Dr. J" Erving with a 123–107 victory that clinched the title.

Johnson was named MVP of the Finals. He became the first rookie to win that honor. The performance by the 20-year-old superstar heralded a new era in the NBA. He would play a leading role in expanding the league's popularity in the 1980s.

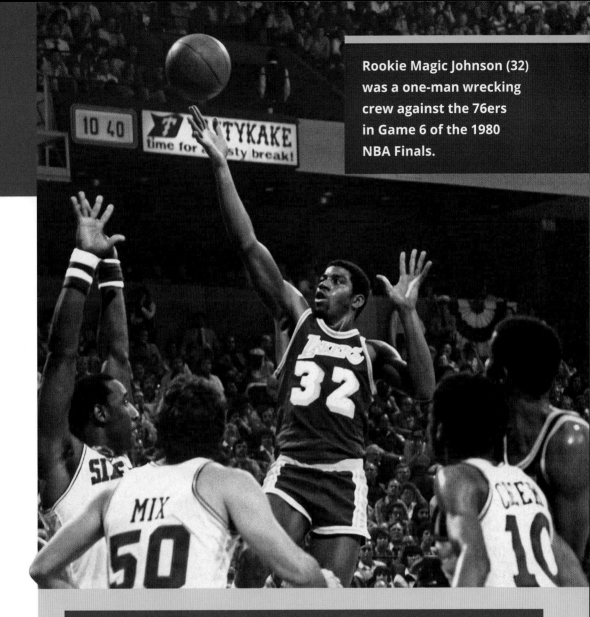

Rookie Magic Johnson (32) was a one-man wrecking crew against the 76ers in Game 6 of the 1980 NBA Finals.

## TAPE DELAY

In 1980 the NBA wasn't as popular as it is today. It sounds hard to believe now, but the series-deciding game of the NBA Finals was shown on tape delay by CBS in most of the country. Game 6 was televised on delay at 11:30 p.m. eastern standard time, two and a half hours after tip-off. Only viewers in Los Angeles and Philadelphia saw it live.

# 05

Cleveland's Kyrie Irving (2) drives past Golden State's Draymond Green for a layup in Game 7 of the 2016 NBA Finals.

## CLEVELAND ROCKS

Game 7 of the 2016 NBA Finals in Oakland, California, was going to be historic one way or another. Golden State, the home team, was trying to defeat Cleveland in a second straight Finals. The Warriors had won an NBA-record 73 games in the regular season and wanted to cap that achievement with a championship.

The Cavaliers, meanwhile, were attempting to win their first title. Moreover, they had a chance to capture the first pro sports crown for the city of Cleveland since the Browns were the National Football League (NFL) champions in 1964. The Cavs also could become the first team to rally from a 3–1 series deficit to win the NBA Finals.

LeBron James has an armful of hardware as he and the Cavaliers celebrate their first NBA championship.

Warriors forward Draymond Green started Game 7 at Oracle Arena with a hot hand. He hit all five of his three-pointers and scored 22 points as his team took a 49–42 halftime lead.

The lead then went back and forth through much of the second half. Klay Thompson's layup for the Warriors tied the score 89–89 with 4:39 left. But then neither team scored for nearly four minutes.

It looked like Golden State would change that on a fast break with less than two minutes to play. Warriors guard Stephen Curry fed teammate Andre Iguodala, who was streaking down the lane. But LeBron James came flying in from behind and swatted away Iguodala's layup attempt.

With just over a minute to play, the Cavs got the ball to guard Kyrie Irving. As the shot clock ticked down, he launched a three-pointer from the wing. The 25-footer went in with 53 seconds remaining, giving Cleveland a 92–89 lead.

The Cavaliers held on to win 93–89. James racked up 27 points, 11 rebounds, and 11 assists and was named Finals MVP.

# 04

# CHAMBERLAIN SCORES 100

Radio announcer Bill Campbell shouted, "It's good! He made it! That's 100!" He was calling the radio play-by-play of the Philadelphia Warriors' game against the New York Knicks on March 2, 1962. The Warriors' Wilt Chamberlain set the NBA single-game scoring record that night with an incredible 100 points. A crowd of 4,124 was on hand for the game at Hershey Sports Arena in Hershey, Pennsylvania.

From the opening tip, the Warriors and Chamberlain were in command. By the end of the first quarter, the 7-foot-1 center had scored 23 points. At halftime, Philadelphia led 79–68. Chamberlain had scored 41. The Warriors' players decided they would make even more of an effort to get the ball in his hands in the second half.

Wilt Chamberlain scores his 100th point of the night on March 2, 1962.

# A NIGHT OF RECORDS

In his big game on March 2, 1962, Wilt Chamberlain also set NBA records for field goals attempted (63) and made (36), free throws made (28), and most points in a quarter (31) and a half (59). Normally a poor free-throw shooter, Chamberlain connected on 28 of 32 tries that night.

"Wilt the Stilt" had scored an NBA-record 78 points in a game earlier that season. He blew past that with almost eight minutes left in the game. With a minute remaining, Chamberlain's total stood at 98 points. He then missed two shots. But the Warriors got both rebounds. Forward Joe Ruklick passed to Chamberlain. He dunked in his 99th and 100th points with 46 seconds left! Fans ran onto the court to celebrate. The Warriors won 169–147.

For the 1961–62 season, Chamberlain averaged 50.4 points per game. This is still easily the NBA record.

# 03

## REED'S RETURN

**N**ew York Knicks fans had reasons to be worried before Game 7 of the 1970 NBA Finals. After all, their team was coming off a 135–113 road loss to the Los Angeles Lakers in Game 6. The Knicks played that game without center and captain Willis Reed. He had suffered a torn thigh muscle in New York's victory in Game 5. Without Reed, the MVP of the regular season and All-Star Game that year, the Knicks had looked helpless against Lakers big man Wilt Chamberlain, who scored 45 points in Game 6.

Nobody knew whether Reed would be able to play in the series finale back in New York. When the Knicks took the court for pregame warm-ups before Game 7, Reed remained in the locker room at Madison Square Garden.

Just before the opening tip, the burly 6-foot-9 center limped through the tunnel and onto the court. He was going to give it a shot.

Reed left no doubt who was No. 1 after his dramatic Game 7 performance.

Reed lined up across from Chamberlain for the opening tip. He then scored the Knicks' first two baskets on jump shots. They would be his only points of the game. But by playing through pain, he inspired his team and helped it race to a big lead. He also defended Chamberlain, holding the 7-foot-1 giant to just 21 points.

Reed's stats for the night—four points and three rebounds—were not impressive. But "he gave us a tremendous lift, just going out there," New York coach Red Holzman said afterward.

New York guard Walt Frazier picked up the slack on offense, finishing with 36 points and 19 assists. The Knicks rolled to a 113–99 win and clinched their first NBA title. Reed was named Finals MVP following a gutsy performance that made him an NBA legend.

**02**

Michael Jordan takes his final shot as a Chicago Bull, a game-winning jumper against the Utah Jazz in Game 6 of the 1998 NBA Finals.

# MJ GOES 6-FOR-6

**M**ichael Jordan had done this before. The man widely considered the NBA's greatest player ever had led the Chicago Bulls to the NBA Finals for the sixth time in 1998. They'd won the first five. Now, with a 3–2 series lead over the Utah Jazz, Jordan was one victory away from grabbing a sixth ring.

But Utah had home-court advantage in the Finals and a late lead in Game 6. If the Jazz could close it out, they'd host a winner-take-all Game 7 in Salt Lake City. Jordan had no interest in letting that happen.

Utah's John Stockton hit a three-pointer with 41.8 seconds remaining to give the Jazz an 86–83 lead. Jordan took over from there. First, the 35-year-old shooting guard drove in for a layup with 37.1 seconds left to bring his team within one point. Then, with 21 seconds remaining, he stripped the ball away from Utah forward Karl Malone.

Jordan dribbled up the court. He tried to shake off Utah's Bryon Russell with a crossover move at the top of the key. Russell fell off balance. Jordan rose and shot a 20-footer that swished in with 5.2 seconds left. The Bulls were ahead by a point. Jordan held his follow-through with his right arm raised as the Delta Center crowd was silenced.

Stockton missed Utah's final shot, and Chicago had an 87–86 victory. The iconic shot by Jordan would be his last in a Chicago uniform. He finished Game 6 with 45 points and received his sixth Finals MVP honor.

It capped the Bulls' dynasty and was the end of an era. Jordan's career had many memorable moments, but it's hard to top the sight of him sinking the game-winning jumper against the Jazz.

# 01

# TRIPLE-OT THRILLER

**F**ans at Boston Garden got more than their money's worth from Game 5 of the 1976 NBA Finals. The contest between the Boston Celtics and the Phoenix Suns featured enough twists and turns for a whole series.

The title round matched the tradition-steeped Celtics and the young upstarts from Phoenix. The Suns franchise was just eight years old and had joined the NBA through league expansion. Boston, on the other hand, was one of the NBA's original teams when the league was formed in the 1940s.

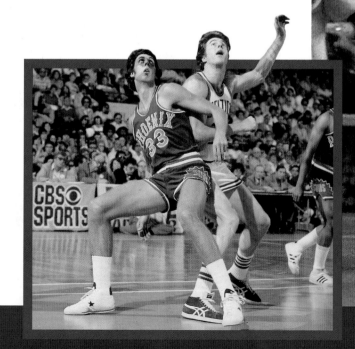

Phoenix center Alvan Adams battles for position against Boston's Dave Cowens during Game 5 of the 1976 NBA Finals.

The teams split the first four games, making Game 5 crucial. And when the Suns rallied from a 15-point halftime deficit to force overtime at 95–95, the excitement was just getting started.

Each team scored six points in the first overtime. With time running out, forward Paul Silas signaled that he wanted a Celtics timeout. One problem: Boston had no timeouts left. Referee Richie Powers ignored Silas. According to the rules, the Celtics should have been assessed a technical foul and the Suns awarded a free throw. The Suns' coaches fumed on the sideline.

The second overtime brought more drama. The Celtics led by three with 15 seconds remaining. With no three-point line yet in the NBA, the Suns would need to score twice. And that's what they did. A Suns basket followed by a Paul Westphal steal and a basket by Curtis Perry put Phoenix up 110–109 with four seconds left.

Not to be outdone, Boston's John Havlicek raced the length of the floor and made a 15-foot bank shot. The Garden went wild. Hundreds of fans stormed onto the floor. But the game was not over. The officials put one second back on the clock and prepared to give Phoenix the ball.

At that point, Westphal had what turned out to be a brilliant idea. He asked for a timeout that he knew his team did not have. This resulted in a one-shot technical foul. Jo Jo White sank the free throw to extend the Celtics' lead to 112–110. But it allowed the Suns to inbound the ball from midcourt rather than having to go the length of the court in one second.

The inbounds pass went to forward Gar Heard. Standing several feet beyond the top of the key, he released a high turnaround shot. It went in, stunning the Garden faithful and the Celtics players. The score was tied 112–112. The game headed to a third overtime.

With key players on both teams having fouled out, a seldom-used reserve, second-year forward Glenn McDonald, came through for the Celtics. He scored six of his team's 16 points in the third overtime. Boston finally pulled out an exhausting 128–126 victory.

"That was the most exciting basketball game I've ever seen," said Hall of Famer Rick Barry, who covered it as part of the television broadcast crew. "They just had one great play after another."

The game is one of only two in NBA Finals history to last three overtimes. Two days later, the Celtics defeated the Suns 87–80 in Phoenix to clinch their 13th NBA championship. And they didn't need overtime to do it.

**With a hand in his face, Suns forward Gar Heard sent the game into triple-overtime with his long jump shot.**

# HONORABLE MENTIONS

**CELTICS 125, HAWKS 123:** Rookie center Bill Russell grabbed 32 rebounds and scored 19 points as Boston edged the St. Louis Hawks in double overtime in Game 7 of the 1957 NBA Finals at Boston Garden. The win launched what many consider the league's greatest dynasty ever, as the Celtics won 11 titles in 13 seasons.

**CELTICS 95, LAKERS 93:** Boston held off visiting Los Angeles in Game 7 in 1966 to secure a record eighth straight NBA title. Russell had 25 points and 32 rebounds. The game was Red Auerbach's last as Celtics head coach.

**TRAIL BLAZERS 109, 76ERS 107:** Center Bill Walton's 20 points, 23 rebounds, seven assists, and eight blocks powered host Portland to a Game 6 victory over Julius "Dr. J" Erving and Philadelphia for the 1977 championship.

**PISTONS 186, NUGGETS 184:** Isiah Thomas scored 47 points in a triple-overtime shootout to help visiting Detroit beat Denver on December 13, 1983. It remains the NBA's highest-scoring game ever. Kiki Vandeweghe poured in 51 points and Alex English added 47 for the Nuggets. Detroit's John Long had 41 points as a record four players scored 40 or more in the game.

**LAKERS 111, CELTICS 100:** Series MVP Kareem Abdul-Jabbar, who was 38 years old, scored 29 points as Los Angeles won Game 6 to clinch the 1985 NBA title. The Lakers became the first visiting team to win the title at Boston Garden. It also gave them their first Finals triumph over the Celtics after eight failed tries.

**CELTICS 108, PISTONS 107:** Larry Bird stole Thomas's inbounds pass and fed Dennis Johnson for a go-ahead layup with one second left as Boston edged Detroit in Game 5 of the 1987 Eastern Conference finals at Boston Garden. The Celtics went on to win the series in seven games but lost in the NBA Finals to the Lakers.

**CELTICS 118, HAWKS 116:** In one of the great shot-making duels of all time, Bird scored 20 of his 34 points in the fourth quarter as host Boston nipped Atlanta and Dominique Wilkins in Game 7 of a 1988 Eastern Conference semifinal series. Wilkins finished with 47 points in a losing effort.

**BULLS 101, CAVALIERS 100:** Michael Jordan hung in the air over Craig Ehlo and hit "The Shot," a buzzer-beating jumper that led Chicago past host Cleveland in the deciding Game 5 of their 1989 Eastern Conference first-round series. It was one of 25 game-winners that Jordan made for the Bulls, and the video highlight is one of his most famous.

**PACERS 107, KNICKS 105:** In an incredible sequence, Knicks nemesis Reggie Miller scored eight points in nine seconds—he sank two three-pointers and two free throws—to lead Indiana to a comeback victory at New York in Game 1 of the teams' 1995 Eastern Conference semifinal series. The Pacers won the series in seven games.

# GLOSSARY

**ASSIST**

A pass that leads directly to a scored basket.

**CLUTCH**

Successful in an important or pressure-packed situation.

**CONSECUTIVE**

Following each other without interruption.

**DYNASTY**

An extended period of success, usually involving multiple championships.

**FRANCHISE**

An entire sports organization, including the players, coaches, and staff.

**LEGENDARY**

Regarded as one of the best to ever play.

**MERGE**

To join with another to create something new, such as a company, a team, or a league.

**OVERTIME**

An extra period of play when the score is tied after regulation.

**POINT GUARD**

The player who directs the team's offensive attack.

**ROOKIE**

A first-year player.

**TRIPLE-DOUBLE**

Accumulating 10 or more of three statistical categories in a game, most frequently points, rebounds, and assists.

# MORE INFORMATION

## ONLINE RESOURCES

To learn more about the NBA's greatest games, visit **abdobooklinks.com**. These links are routinely monitored and updated to provide the most current information available.

## BOOKS

Donnelly, Patrick. *The Best NBA Centers of All Time*. Minneapolis, MN: Abdo Publishing, 2015.

Ervin, Phil. *Total Basketball*. Minneapolis, MN: Abdo Publishing, 2017.

Graves, Will. *Make Me the Best Basketball Player*. Minneapolis, MN: Abdo Publishing, 2017.

## PLACE TO VISIT

### NAISMITH MEMORIAL BASKETBALL HALL OF FAME
1000 Hall of Fame Avenue
Springfield, MA 01105
877–446–6752
**hoophall.com**

The Basketball Hall of Fame is like a museum dedicated to basketball. It highlights the greatest players, coaches, and moments in the sport's history. Many of the players mentioned in this book are enshrined there. It is home to more than 300 inductees and more than 40,000 square feet of basketball history.

# INDEX

# ABOUT THE AUTHOR

Matt Tustison is a sports copy editor at the *Washington Post*. He also has worked as a sports copy editor at other newspapers, including the *Palm Beach (Fla.) Post*, and as an editor and writer of children's sports books.